88 More Angels
Elizabeth Doreen Wilder

Photography by Rob Henderson

Published 2020
Text copyright © Elizabeth Doreen Wilder 2020
Photographs copyright © Rob Henderson

ISBN: 978-0-6487976-7-8

Silverbird Publishing
PO Box 72
Eltham Victoria 3095
www.workingtype.com.au/silverbird

Dedicated to Shirley Flett
'An angel among us'

Table of Contents

Introduction		x
1	Auras	1
2	Belief	3
3	Being	5
4	Birthright	7
5	Bringing	9
6	Certainty	11
7	Charm	13
8	Cheerfulness	15
9	Choice	17
10	Clearance	19
11	Compassion	21
12	Cosmic Order	23
13	Curiosity	25
14	Development	27
15	Discovery	29
16	Dreaming	31
17	Empathy	33
18	Empowerment	35
19	Enchantment	37
20	Endurance	39
21	Endings	41
22	Energy	43
23	Enigma	45
24	Eternity	47
25	Etherification	49
26	Excellence	51
27	Excitement	53

28	Expression	55
29	Extension	57
30	Falling Stars	59
31	Feelings	61
32	Forgiveness	63
33	Fulfilment	65
34	Fun	67
35	Gentleness	69
36	Glee	71
37	Gloriousness	73
38	Graciousness	75
39	Grandeur	77
40	Guidance	79
41	Healing	81
42	Heavenliness	83
43	Holiness	85
44	Humility	87
45	Instinct	89
46	Intuition	91
47	Jest	93
48	Kindred-spirits	95
49	Lightness	97
50	Lucidity	99
51	Magnetism	101
52	Majesty	103
53	Miracles	105
54	Mysticism	107
55	Openness	109
56	Outlook	111
57	Past Lives	113
58	Prayer	115

59	Quests	117
60	Radiance	119
61	Recovery	121
62	Reflection	123
63	Regeneration	125
64	Rejoicing	127
65	Release	129
66	Renewal	131
67	Resolution	133
68	Restoration	135
69	Reverence	137
70	Sharing	139
71	Sentiment	141
72	Serendipity	143
73	Serenity	145
74	Spirituality	147
75	Tasks	149
76	Telepathy	151
77	Thought	153
78	Time	155
79	Tolerance	157
80	Tranquillity	159
81	Transcendence	161
82	Translucence	163
83	Triumph	165
84	Unlimited	167
85	Virtue	169
86	Wholeness	171
87	Wistfulness	173
88	Wonder	175

Introduction

How they came to me

When I was a very young, I became fascinated with the view of clouds from my back veranda. I took every opportunity to view them on my way to play in the back yard.

In my first book, *88 Angels*, I describe this in greater detail. For the sake of this, my second book, I wish to introduce some more esoteric concepts of clouds, and angels.

Having gone through a rather serious illness, some 12 years ago now, I was given 6 weeks to live at the time. Well, I amazed all the doctors by not only surviving, but thriving as well. My heart goes out to all those who may be experiencing difficulty, (of any sort), who manage to do what we were all born to do; *overcome*!

This book is for all those valiant enough to face their worst fears and become stronger for becoming victorious over them through their own Angels.

Where did they come from? The certainty of their existence in most branches of history is unprecedented, and it is my belief now, absolutely that they exist among us, around us, with us at all times with unfailing Love, if only we could become more aware of their guidance and presence.

Having studied metaphysics for over 30 years now, I am aware of the unseen vibrations surrounding all of us. It is this heightened awareness that will bring you into touch with your own angels. They have been watching silently over you all your life. They may come in the form of instinct or the intuitive in your choices in life.

Indeed, they may also have unique messages just for you. So use your intuition often, and trust it implicitly. It is always in your best interests for the highest path you can travel this lifetime.

My belief is that the only reason we are born is to develop spiritually. Each in our own way, through experience and the very choices we make for our own lives. And these can always be changed with new choices, clearer thinking and a sense of balance toward the most positive outcomes for our future.

Your Angels need your permission to help you, so call on them as often as you genuinely need them. They *do* need to be requested, so keep this in mind.

Prayers and prayer feedback
Once I became a little more familiar with their energy, I noticed my faith in them grow, and quietly found myself doing, (perhaps as instructed) small rituals when I would hear of someone who was ill or going through some tribulation. One of these was to light a little tee-light candle for the person with their name written on a piece of paper at the top, the date, and the type of help needed. I would 'loan' them some of my Angels for a period to help them along and get through their difficulty.

To my astonishment this *always* worked. My faith grew rapidly in the small but very real service that *any* of us can do with something as simple as a candle and a prayer *directing* the energy of the Angels toward hardship. Anyone's!

By working with your own Angels and the ones in this, '88 More Angels', it is the intention of the author to bring to your life the faith you need to climb any of your own personal mountains (or clouds), and assist others who may be having a little trouble looking up.

Quietude in soul
Before you begin your connection with your own Angels, find a quiet place in your home. It is preferable that you eventually only use this space for your quiet time to connect with yourself, God, Goddess, all that is. Whatever you believe in. No matter what way you experience it, this space is where you will go every day, or whenever you feel the need to 'connect' with Source.

It is the intended by using this book that your own Angels will become familiar to you, and be of comfort to you when you or someone you know or care for, are in need of light.

There are no rules to working with your Angels, except for clarity of mind and a sincere heart. Your intention will always answer your guidance, so it is a very practical idea to be as centred about your intention as possible, and use visualisation to help you.

Visualisation
This is as simple as taking a few relaxing breaths to clear your mind, and emptying it of all thoughts, then visualise the intended person or the things you are blessing with your Angels' energy and then clearly sending that message from the heart. Imagine the person or thing done i.e. the healing already occurred and see the person smiling and without fear.

This, my second work is indeed what I owe my own Angels, and the least I can do in gratitude of them having given me the faith to restore me. It is with the greatest hope that by sharing these beautiful Angels with you or someone you love, that this hope is passed on; in the same way all spirit experiences restoration.

My belief is that all symbology, inclusive of the words you are reading now, are philosophically merely a chain of ideas forged over time and influence. From many languages, symbols and histories, which we absorb into our lives in accordance with our original tribal teachers, our parents, we then expand with our own experiences and cultures throughout the course of our lives.

Indeed, inside each of our cerebral cortex's are 100 trillion neural connectors at work at all times, especially so in the mystery of healing. With this great gift, we all have Angels. This appears to be just another sense to me, or anyone, who has had any Angelic experiences.

They are there, whether acknowledged or not, to guide, safeguard and help us discover the reason we are here. So have a heart and an open mind as you enjoy *88 More Angels*, as they wish to transmit only Love to all, and to reconnect you with your own great Angels who have been watching over you all this time.

So, you may find this book is slightly more esoteric that the first. The intention is that you are made more conscious of the beautiful Angels surrounding you and by so doing; both your life and your own starseed become clearer and stronger.

Good is God with an extra 'o'.
To me the word good is just God with an extra 'o'. When you take a moment to feel your association with this word, you will notice a small but subtle shift

in the way you feel. This is more than merely the power of positive thinking, it is the DNA strand that remembers the word and all its' associations throughout time. Indeed the words' origin is that of Godliness.

Most certainly, we would all love God to be with us all the time. The fact is that 'he/she/all that is in the Universe' is 'with' us all the time. We are the testimony of all our fathers' fathers and mothers' mothers right back to the beginning of humanity on this planet, and even further back to starseed.

Therefore, whatever star seed you are made of, it makes sense that this travels with you from lifetime to lifetime to lifetime, no matter what form your matter takes. It is my belief that this part of us travels with our eternal soul.

May all who share this book become blessed by its' content and the exquisite photography of International Photographer, Rob Henderson.

From my own original star seed come my *88 More Angels* to you, whoever you are, whatever your journey; may they remind you of your true worth in this vast Universe of all possibilities.

1
Auras

Thy swollen spirit
Always near
For wholeness
It is great to have you near
'I am the Angel of Auras'

2
Belief

'You can take me -
Or leave me'
Wherever you wish!

By doing both –
You give me bliss...
'I am the Angel of Belief'

3
Being

You will have me –
Or not
From the beginning
Till end,
Nevertheless, I am the only –
Deeply felt friend.
'I am the Angel of Being'

4
Birthright

Never to be forgotten
Remember not to forget,
What you're originally given
Cannot be taken from this,

Thy soul is a great vessel,
In whom life's journey will travel,
And the joy of it all,
Is how it unravels.
'I am the Angel of Birth-right'

5
Bringing

Treasure your treasure
It is your own indeed
Moreover, remember to ask for me
Whenever in need

You lack nothing at all
Moreover, there is nothing amiss
Its' just where value left it,
Waiting to be blessed!
'I am the Angel of Bringing'

88 MORE ANGELS

6
Certainty

When in doubt you must call for me.
I am always quite near,
With those runaway thoughts
I will expel all the fear.

I am right by you
Just feel 'turnaround' here,
For your confidence I keep,
Close to my heart, my Dear.
'I am the Angel of Certainty'

12   88 MORE ANGELS

7
Charm

You see thy continence
Is purely sweet
Thy charms like bracelets
Such pretty treats
She is from giving
With smiles galore
This is the truth of her
Charm some more
'I am the Angel of Charm'

14   88 MORE ANGELS

8
Cheerfulness

Sunshine is emerging...
So beautiful – so bright...
To feel the dawn
Of the days' new light...

So do listen, sweet child
With your mind and your heart
And each new day
Is a brand new start!
'I am the Angel of Cheerfulness'

16   88 MORE ANGELS

9
Choice

Ode nought to this
Thy hand and robe –
As paths unravel
Fate will be known!

By this or that path
They are but one and the same.
Thy choices strong,
Are but what remain.
'I am the Angel of Choice'

18   88 MORE ANGELS

10
Clearance

From one day to the next
All eternal throng...
We are dancing in Universes
Of our own song...

Complete as you go
And you will never rush
For the clear are the strong
In yourself have great trust!
'I am the Angel of Clearance'

20   88 MORE ANGELS

11
Compassion

Presence of thine
Composure in the dark
For all who need me now
My light a gracious spark

There is no soul who is left
Without another to protect
They will make themselves known to you
Keep a close watch always
For all little clues...
'I am the Angel of Compassion'

12
Cosmic Order

Bluer than cornflowers
Thy mystery bright...
Closer to the edge
Of the cosmic light

In all cosmic order –
Vibrations upon
The valley of syzergy
We all travel on...
'I am the Angel of Cosmic Order'

88 MORE ANGELS

13
Curiosity

I have travelled with adventures
Across all the great lands...
Of the Great Mother Earth
Within all commands...

That you travel and see,
All you are to see now...
Within Gods' eyes,
Your eternal vow...
'I am the Angel of Curiosity'

88 MORE ANGELS

14
Development

Your growth and I
Are intertwined
And fixed within
Your greatness lies
Await not a second
Your lifetime now
'I am the Angel of Development'

88 MORE ANGELS

15
Discovery

From rooftop to fountain,
You will eternally display
Your love of my assistance
In every way

So think of me daily
As you stride forward to the new
I'm a gift always present
In most adventurous you!
'I am the Angel of Discovery'

88 MORE ANGELS

16
Dreaming

On gossamer wings
Sprinkling stardust afar
You know I look after
Your dreaming thus far.

So keep me under your pillow
With lavender grace
Best dreams are my wishes
As you sleep from awake...
'I am the Angel of Dreaming'

17
Empathy

Drawn of a vessel,
This cup of heart round,
Spilling the sharing
To glory you are bound...

Empathy clearly
Takes not years to know...
In its' nature all beauty
Forever bestowed...
'I am the Angel of Empathy'

88 MORE ANGELS

18
Empowerment

To they wilfulness glory
'You can do it' you see!
Just keep trying harder
Until you only see me…

No person shall have it
Unless you give it away
This gift is your own
To the end of your days
'I am the Angel of Empowerment'

19
Enchantment

Full of my charm
You will curious be
As the essence of soul
Enraptured in me

Forget not my beauty
Abound to delight
I will always be with you
Throughout all of your life!
'I am the Angel of Enchantment'

88 MORE ANGELS

20
Endurance

When you feel you have reached
The journeys' end
With nothing more
To give or defend

When the fight has left
In addition, you need a friend
I will be with thee
To enable strength

Carry thy spirit
As anew
Without the burdens
To dust they will shoo!
'I am the Angel of Endurance'

88 MORE ANGELS

21
Endings

Though ending seem
To make you sad
They are just new beginnings
New experience to have

To help your soul
Grow rich on the path
Many of these
Is a blessed mark
'I am the Angel of Endings'

88 MORE ANGELS

22
Energy

All things contain me,
All creation of this –
Your task is to know me,
In all of thy bliss,

I give all indications,
And sometimes a kiss,
You are made of me completely,
Please know this…
'I am the Angel of Energy'

44   88 MORE ANGELS

23
Enigma

Though many of these
One-lifetime counts
The mystery encountered
Is worth the route

God placed these puzzles
In all your hands
To help you grow
To understand
'I am the Angel of Enigma'

88 MORE ANGELS

24
Eternity

At the time of your birth
I am present to all
Where times' mists have enveloped
Your soul evermore

I am still with you always
Try not to forget –
In that thought will, you capture
Your ultimate best
'I am the Angel of Eternity'

25
Etherification

That you are an enigma
From birth till dust
And the mystery of you
You have to trust

Knowing that there's no limit
For there's no limit here...
Existence is stronger...
When this becomes clear...
'I am the Angel of Etherification'

26
Excellence

By your hand –
And by my Grace
As each to find –
Their proper place.

Refine me and know
That all dreams become clear
By your standard you will grow
By your side, I'll stay near!
'I am the Angel of Excellence'

88 MORE ANGELS

27
Excitement

Our whirling dervish
Inexplicable bliss
Is uncontainable
And ne'er to be missed

We play your imaginings
To bring them to life!
This journey is your right
Without any strife
'I am the Angel of Excitement'

28
Expression

Show me every emotion
Come express yourself dear!
Art, dance, music, theatre...
Yes! And even your tears...

My range is enormous
So go with it you see...
For your aptitude will keep me near!
'I am the Angel of Expression'

88 MORE ANGELS

29
Extension

Your walls are but invisible
Maybe you do not see
Through our eyes.
All is joined and
Extension is ease

So think with your third eye
Yet close but the two
And closer to us
Will be every view
'I am the Angel of Extension'

88 MORE ANGELS

30
Falling Stars

We appear to those
Whose hearts in need
Who need a wish?
Into that wish we breathe

That falling star
Before your eyes
Is yours' alone
As we've designed
'I am the Angel of Falling Stars'

31
Feelings

Tune into me now
I am the truth of all chatter...
Forget all the outside
It is me that most matters.

If you follow me closely
You will see you're in synch.
For with these you are powerful
Whole and can think!
'I am the Angel of Feelings'

32
Forgiveness

We challenge most
To learn us well
For all that follows
Is of the light
Without this you
May feel in the dark or alone
However, with it everything is known.
'I am the Angel of Forgiveness'

64   88 MORE ANGELS

33
Fulfilment

You may work all of a lifetime,
Or only one day –
In me, you see glory
As champions', pray.

All the glitter and fun
Of tasks well done here.
Once your love of what you do
Becomes finally clear...
I am the Angel of Fulfilment!'

34
Fun

In more laughter
Am I light to dark?
In an open heart
Find most delight
Uplift thy spirit
When feeling glum
'I am the Angel of Fun'

88 MORE ANGELS

35
Gentleness

So softly, I gather,
From the corners of Love,
To treat you with such grace
Known only to doves.

You will feel me in heartstrings,
As I pluck them so pure,
As all gather at evening,
Your peace to ensure!
'I am the Angel of Gentleness'

36
Glee

When sadness prevails
I come visit at once...
As the laughter is needed
More than any nuance...

From your sorrow
Transported
To cheerful with bliss
My puns are intended
I make sure I don't miss!
'I am the Angel of Glee'

37
Gloriousness

For God hath one path
For all – sweet child…
That path of gentility
Curious – yet mild…

Do not sway
From thy path or ever regret….
Taking the one
Where God is met…
'I am the Angel of Gloriousness'

38
Graciousness

You will feel me near
When you toss your cloak
Over water for women
Or more feeble folk.

My cup runneth over
With understanding you see,
For with this the whole world
Is for you and for me!
'I am thy Angel of Graciousness'

88 MORE ANGELS

39
Grandeur

In golden carriages,
I delight in my play.
You see, I see all things
Just that way.

From jewellery to palaces,
I am most welcome here,
Where the glory of my sight
Stays all the more clear!
'I am the Angel of Grandeur"

40
Guidance

Under Heavens' glow
Our clouds run free
To the bursts of Angels'
Love for thee!

When darkness bursts
Upon your light
My guidance with you
Renewing light...

The rose of Love
Will burn so bright
All burden lifted
Renewed of sight...
'I am the Angel of Guidance'

88 MORE ANGELS

41
Healing

I pour the light on depth of feeling
To ascertain the light of healing
Within you all, it is complete
Your power in it - destined to meet
'I am the Angel of Healing'

88 MORE ANGELS

42
Heavenliness

Such a rush around world
Seems to take me away
Be assured little Angels
I am here and I stay

To free your spirit
To make you clear
As in Gods' heart
You are ever near
'I am the Angel of Heavenliness'

84   88 MORE ANGELS

43
Holiness

Put thy faith in God
And God alone...
You will never
Ever feel forlorn...

Of this assurance,
I give thee this day...
Protection and comfort
If thou follow the way...
'I am the Angel of Holiness'

88 MORE ANGELS

44
Humility

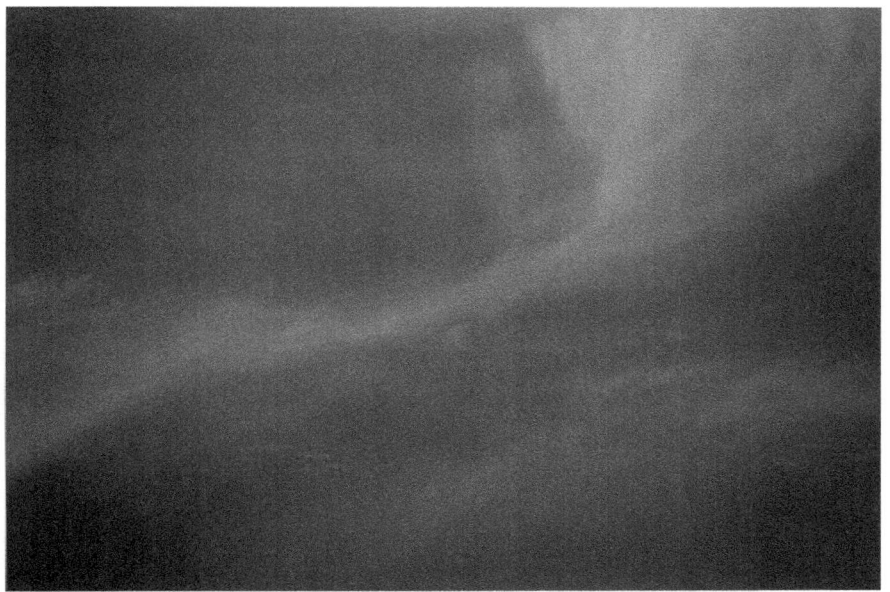

Pouring through each soul
Is always given
Ability to see
What's hidden

Your call to others
Is but a call to self
You are all one
Within your help
'I am the Angel of Humility'

88 MORE ANGELS

45
Instinct

Use me with your wisdom
Intact – and as a level,
I cannot be destroyed
By anything dishevelled!

I am your most primitive past
Yet your sharpest tool,
And when used with your knowledge
You will be nobody's fool!
'I am the Angel of Instinct'

46
Intuition

Profound are we
Your truth we tell
In all you feel
Knowingness dwells

This is your gift
To use at will
It whispers truth
Till you know it still
'I am the Angel of Intuition'

88 MORE ANGELS

47
Jest

I am lurking in corners,
Laughter being my veil –
I come only to cheer you
When dark winds prevail.

My Love is of laughter,
The heartier, the better,
And if you're telling the joke,
I'll be there – to the letter!
'I am the Angel of Jest'

48
Kindred-spirits

You'll know when you have found one
And the many – the more
Uplifted spirits
You will find you adore!

You have known them forever
As they have known you
They await recognition
As you will too!
'I am the Angel of Kindred-spirits'

49
Lightness

In glories' wake
I am all around...
You need but open
To my sight and sound...

You touch and you feel me
In every moment
A feather your testimony
Of all you can show it!
'I am the Angel of Lightness'

88 MORE ANGELS

50
Lucidity

You will know us
By your joyous uplifted realms...
Into your very soul
We have certainly melded...

As all becomes immortal
So crystalline clear
You will feel our presence
So ever, near
'I am the Angel of Lucidity'

88 MORE ANGELS

51
Magnetism

I reflect unto you
Wherever there's need...
I am everywhere
Unto gravity, my seed...

In electrics and wires,
I dance in these things...
If you use me for healing
Much Loving I bring
'I am the Angel of Magnetism'

52
Majesty

From the distant mist
Of ancestral realms...
Into this present day
We always melt...

Our glory is in
All joyful moments –
Of pomp and ceremony
We come in torrents...
'I am the Angel of Majesty'

53
Miracles

Light is not contained...
But sheds and grows
Through spirits' wings
Until all Love- flows...

Eternally yours
When open you are...
I await your pleasure
You command this star!
'I am the Angel of Miracles!'

54
Mysticism

As the ancient ones
Slowly watch all...
We bring to you mystery
Tales of 'other worlds' call...

In tenderness, we embrace you,
The one and the all...
For your mysteries remain
Known to us overall...
'I am the Angel of Mysticism'

55
Openness

Like a handbag – kept open
Linger with me - too long
And you will lovingly see
Mine – the only song.

With eyes constantly open
By the joy I bring in,
I am new ideas brilliant
Honesty lives in this thing!
'I am the Angel of Openness'

110   88 MORE ANGELS

56
Outlook

Look up every morning
As you awaken to light
For your future looks good
It is better and bright…

Let me shine on you now,
For all things are changing
With me you go further
It's the best I'm arranging!
'I am the Angel of Outlook'

57
Past Lives

Since before time began,
I have held you near.
Through swollen centuries –
Gone by and Dear.
For all of your life-times -
I have known you well.
'I am the Angel of Past Lives'

58
Prayer

As you kneel at an alter,
With your hands clasped tight...
Think of me as your shield
Used by day and by night.

I am instantly guided
By your Loving song,
As I hear every voice...
To your prayer I belong!
'I am the Angel of Prayer'

59
Quests

No matter thy task
I am always at hand,
You need but ask for me
At your given command

Hold true to your promise,
All those ones to yourself
I'll fulfil all your dreams,
Into reality they'll melt!
'I am the Angel of Quests'

88 MORE ANGELS

60
Radiance

I spring into action...
Full of light and glee
At the centre of rainbows
There is plenty of me...

When you are peaceful you'll feel me,
I'm an endless pure glow,
In your heart I have faith
This you already know!
'I am the Angel of Radiance'

61
Recovery

When you're unsure of the correct step –
I will guide you to the next...
Have great faith as your allie
For with me you progress.

As small as
That next step may be...
It's the trying that's been,
It is the mountain of effort
I truly see...
'I am the Angel of Recovery'

62
Reflection

Water my mirror –
Light waves are the transport
Sun, moon – my perfection
In Heavens' constant glow.

Your mirrors adorn me,
As I dance in your light,
Oh vision! 'pon vision –
My purest delight!
'I am the Angel of Reflection'

88 MORE ANGELS

63
Regeneration

In a walk or a swim
Or health treatment as well,
I give you the betterment
Only trying will tell....

Where the old becomes new
Where your body regrows,
I am in all your being
Right down to your toes!
'I am the Angel of Regeneration'

64
Rejoicing

From the start to the end
And wherever you go –
I will always be with you
Surely you already know.

When life comes back from a beating
Comes back to life after a low…
I am the feeling that guides you,
Opens heart – To your growth…
'I am the Angel of Rejoicing'

88 MORE ANGELS

65
Release

So keep faith
When infirm...
As I teach you
To relearn...

All your holding
Let go
For your keeping
The next growth!
'I am the Angel of Release'

88 MORE ANGELS

66
Renewal

Eternal as you are...
Ever changing in mood,
I am sure to be with you
To calm and to soothe...

Refreshing each cell
Ever changing they be...
You need to look to your attitude
And there you'll find me!
'I am the Angel of Renewal'

88 MORE ANGELS

67
Resolution

Stand firm and strong,
We will give you the strength...
To carry on – once all seems spent...

It is within you all to hold fast and win!
From poor to rich form stirrings within...

Your knowledge breaths-the breath of courage...
To know beyond what's begged or borrowed...

I am always with you
When you need me the most...
Without ego – without need
Of charm or boast!
'I am the Angel of Resolution'

68
Restoration

From the old comes the new
With most loving of care,
The scent of beeswax
Is usually there.

So restore to its' glory
For time ticks further on...
As your spirit renews
With each passing sun!
I am the Angel of Restoration!

69
Reverence

I am seen
In that spark of grace,
Most lucid moments
Of time or space.

In beauty I warm –
Full of hearts' greatest light
In gentleness, soften
All darkness to bright!

I come tenderly
As the truth of the dove,
Adorning your spirit –
Its' everlasting Love!
'I am the Angel of Reverence'

70
Sharing

By giving you learn
That there's more than your lot,
So do it as often
As you must. Never stop!

For in this one thing
Your spirit is measured,
And the growth of your Love,
Is happily boundless!
'I am the Angel of Sharing'

71
Sentiment

I will pierce at your heartstrings
As I play as your muse,
That old music box
Is to me the whole truth

In a favourite old picture,
Is where I will lay
So your heart soars with me
Every night, every day!
'I am the Angel of Sentiment'

.

72
Serendipity

Skipping lightly
Along any street,
I am the one
You are bound to meet.

Your' lightness infuses
Most other souls'
Like streams to rivers
Oh! How your light flows!

And when you are near me
Hats tip whilst you walk by,
The beam so strong
And wide and high...
'I am the Angel of Serendipity'

73
Serenity

In peace's arms,
I quietly wait,
For I know you'll arrive
Just like Heaven's gate.

In the quietest moments
I feel you ablush
And I know you've arrived
By the bliss in the hush.
'I am the Angel of Serenity'

74
Spirituality

From the North to the South
I am practised by day,
And in regions unknown
By night I'm at play

My message abounds,
As the eternity now,
And to enjoy my pleasures
You can start, you know how!
'I am the Angel of Spirituality'

75
Tasks

The work is a breeze.
Disappears fast.
For I am around
To clear up the past.

With broom and with mop
Or computer too,
I will lift all your burdens
By helping you do...
'I am the Angel of Tasks'

76
Telepathy

What thought couldn't show you
My presence prevails,
To guide you right through
The 'going off' rails.

All knowledge within me,
'Thoughts are things' don't you know!
And wherever you are
Most surely I'll go!
'I am the Angel of Telepathy'

88 MORE ANGELS

77
Thought

I wander about,
From one to the other...
But, get me in alignment
And your mind is a flutter

I pick up and put down,
At the whim of distraction,
In essence, I am here,
For your satisfaction!
'I am the Angel of Thought'

78
Time

Brought forth to change it-
Have no fear of Love...
No tale too small to surround it...
You are part of the dove...
The holiest light surrounds all now
With the present moment-Gods' pure flow...

When light is transformed
So, you teach what you learn,
For spiritual sanction
To Heaven you turn...

The wheels of time
Speeding up…speeding down…
All for Gods' purest witness
In blessings, we're crowned!
'I am the Angel of Time'

79
Tolerance

When you're visiting others
I am surely a must...
As with my full company
You will gain their trust.

There are many who need me,
Quick smart and worldwide,
For with me you will find
You'll create many smiles!
'I am the Angel of Tolerance'

80
Tranquillity

Applied in still waters...
Droplets running from leaves...
Or the solemnest statues,
Where incense burns in the breeze.

I am the peace deep inside you,
I am ever so true,
For my Love is in finding
The greatest - in you!
'I am the Angel of Tranquillity

81
Transcendence

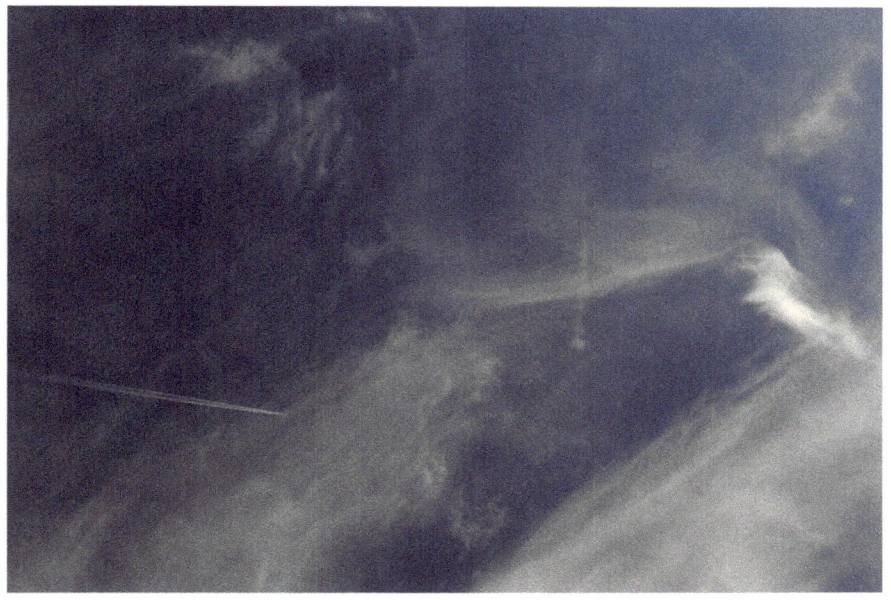

Beams surround you
From your lotus flowers sent...
All the misery of the world
You will eventually transcend

Your light never tiring
Soul gets very clear...
For within all your wiring,
Love overcomes fear.

So look well to your teachers
They are knights of the soul...
And the clearing commenced
Will encourage your growth
'I am the Angel of Transcendence'

82
Translucence

Sunlight through leaves
Those golden rays
On water shimmering
I gaze through all
As they are just the light
Of transparence to me
'I am the Angel of Translucence'

83
Triumph

Though you may not envisage
All my compliments here,
I have always been with you
In each sporting cheer.

I'm the victory intact,
For the doing worth doing,
And my company is loved
At the Finish – get to it!
I am the Angel of Triumph

88 MORE ANGELS

84
Unlimited

I know no boundaries
As I run through eternity,
As the mists out of nowhere –
I am everywhere you see...

There has never been my equal,
For there are none in the Universe
And my Love for you eternal,
As you travel paths of learning...
'I am the Angel of the Unlimited'

85
Virtue

You need never fear losing
For your purity is found
If you keep this thought with you
I'll make things come round.

In essence I am you,
If your spirit could see,
For the utterance is all,
You need to bring me!
'I am the Angel of Virtue'

86
Wholeness

In herbal fusion I hide
Rich grains and good cheer
For the Love of your health
With skin pure and clear.

I'll put roses in cheeks,
And bloom as you grow,
For with me you will flourish
With the foods I will show.
'I am the Angel of Wholeness'

87
Wistfulness

Looking up at the stars
Or the moon, give wonder
Or the rolling green hills,
Or the sound of the thunder

In a flower I'm felt,
In the Love of the heart,
As pounding first Love
Like a waterfall - starts!
I am the Angel of Wistfulness

88 MORE ANGELS

88
Wonder

Thy journey is mine...
With distinguished delight.
By day I assist you
And in dreaming at night

Your smile is my heart-song
My only pure joy
For you only happiness
My heart can implore...

So take your mind on its' journeys,
With these - I'll assist,
As to have you wonder,
Gives me ultimate bliss!
'I am the Angel of Wonder'

www.ingramcontent.com/pod-product-compliance
Lightning Source LLC
Chambersburg PA
CBHW051537010526
44107CB00064B/2758